Buggly Bear's
HICCUP Cure

Buggly Bear's HICCUP Cure

by True Kelley

Parents Magazine Press • New York

Copyright © 1982 by True Kelley
All rights reserved.
Printed in the United States of America.
10 9 8 7 6 5 4 3

Library of Congress Cataloging in Publication Data
Kelley, True. Buggly Bear's hiccup cure.
Summary: Forrest Moose tries every way he can
think of to cure Buggly's hiccups.
[1. Hiccups—Fiction. 2. Animals—Fiction.]
I. Title.
PZ7.K2824Bu [E] 81-16903
ISBN 0-8193-1081-6 AACR2
ISBN 0-8193-1082-4 (lib. bdg.)

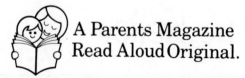 A Parents Magazine
Read Aloud Original.

For the "rents", Adelaide and Mark Kelley

Buggly Bear woke up from his winter nap
with a start!
He had the hiccups.

He had a very bad case

of the hiccups.

"Hiccups!" said his friend Forrest.
"I know lots of cures."

"Hic?" said Buggly.

"Hold your breath while I
count to 100," said Forrest.

"1, 2, 3, 4, 5, 6, 7, 8, 9, 10,"
counted Forrest.
But Forrest wasn't very good
at counting over 10.
"14...20...37," he went on.

"Ummm...33...62...42...

89...90...56...100!"

"HIC!" said Buggly.

"Hang upside down and drink a bucket
of honey," suggested Forrest.

"Hic, gurgle, hic!" said Buggly.

"Tickle, tickle, tickle!" said Forrest.

"Hee, hee, hee, hic!
Hee, hee, hic!" laughed Buggly.

"Eat three loaves of Moose-Moss Bread," said Forrest.

"Maybe if I sit on your stomach,"
said Forrest.

"HIC!" said Buggly.

"If you just forget about your hiccups,
they'll go away.
A little song and dance will
get your mind off them," said Forrest.

Forrest's song began:
    "Oh, do the mooshy-mashy,
    Eat potatoes squishy-squashy.
    Lunchtime will be soon,
    Underneath the moo-moo-moon!"

Forrest danced wildly
through twenty-seven more verses.

But it didn't work.

"Hic," said Buggly.

"Hypnosis!" said Forrest.
"Your eyelids are growing *heavy*...
  You are in my *pow—er-r-r*.
  You are a chicken!"
"Cluck," said Buggly.
"You are a chicken WITHOUT hiccups,"
  said Forrest.

"Cluck-Hic!" said Buggly.

"I will not give up!" said Forrest.
"I will scare them out of you.
What would scare a bear?"

"**BOO!**" said Forrest.

"I hate this!" said Buggly.

Forrest tried his monster costume next.

"...Wait a minute," Buggly said.
"I think...they're...gone..."

"RATS!" he said.

"If this doesn't work, nothing will,"
  said Forrest.
"Swim back and forth across the river
  twenty times."

"Hic," said Buggly tiredly.

Just then Forrest slipped on a
wet rock and fell into the water.
"Help! Help!" he yelled.
"I can't swim!"
The current swept him
towards Headache Falls.

Buggly jumped into the water
after Forrest and swam
out towards him.
Forrest was almost at the edge
of the Falls.

Buggly grabbed him by the horns
just in time!
He dragged Forrest back to shore.

"Thanks," gasped Forrest.

Suddenly Buggly sat up.
"My hiccups are GONE!" he yelled.
"They are REALLY GONE!"

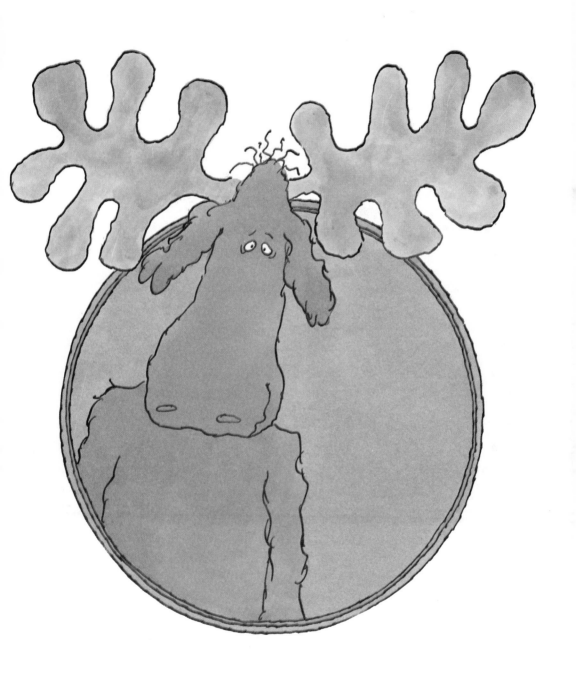

Forrest smiled weakly…

"Hic," said Forrest.

About the Author/Artist

TRUE KELLEY has illustrated many text books and picture books, including CLARA JOINS THE CIRCUS for Parents Magazine Press.

About BUGGLY BEAR'S HICCUP CURE, Ms. Kelley says, "I have now decided that it is easier to live with hiccups than to live with the cures! I personally had the hiccups 27 times while working on this book."

True Kelley lives with her husband in New Hampshire.